THE ADVENTURES OF

Billy the Invisible Bee

BY Ian Ventress

First published in Great Britain as a softback original in 2020

Copyright ©Ian Ventress

The moral right of this author has been asserted.

All rights reserved.

No part of this publication may be reproduced, stored in a retrieval system, or transmitted, in any form or by any means, without the prior permission in writing of the publisher, nor be otherwise circulated in any form of binding or cover other than that in which it is published and without a similar condition including this condition being imposed on the subsequent purchaser.

Typeset in New Century Schoolbook

Editing, design, typesetting and publishing by UK Book Publishing
www.ukbookpublishing.com

ISBN: 978-1-913179-67-0

Can you find my honey pot in every chapter?

INTRODUCTION

Billy the Invisible Bee

Hi I'm called Ben and I'm gonna tell you some tales,

about Billy the invisible bee

We go around helping anyone in need, if we can, Billy and me

If anyone's in trouble they shout out his name

All different adventures, never the same

He needs to keep his honey levels topped up high

Or the magic wears off and you'll see Billy fly

You can hear the buzzing of his tiny wings

He may be a bee but he never stings

He needs the honey so he can prolong

To keep him invisible and fast and strong

So listen to my stories and you will find

That Billy the bee is one of a kind

So keep an eye on Billy, he's the only one

Where he's there one minute, and the next he's gone.

CHAPTER 1

The Fox

Billy heard a shout come through the air

He's got special hearing underneath his fur

A girl shouted for Billy the bee

So we went to see her, Billy and me

"There's a fox," she said, "comes around at night

Comes in my garden gives my bunny a fright

He stands at the cage mouth open wide

If you can't help me I'll have to take him inside."

Billy sat, and had a thought

"Don't worry about your rabbit," he said, "I will sort."

Billy waited, late at night

He waited for the fox to give him a fright

In the garden there were scattered toys

Then in the bushes, Billy heard a noise

Here comes the fox to get the bunny

Billy waited and drank lots of honey

He looked in the cage, got down on one knee

but Billy had lots of honey, so the fox couldn't see

Billy jumped off the fence and sat on his nose

The fox got a shock, he stood and froze

Then Billy buzzed in the fox's ear

You could see in his eyes, there was fear

So the bunny would never be his prey

So scared and shaken he ran away

So that was a lesson the fox had learned

Billy did sort and he never returned.

CHAPTER 2

Injured wing

A boy shouted for Billy, about an injured bird

We've been so busy this week, this was our third

We went in the garden, it couldn't move its wing

It was all tangled up, wrapped around it was some string

If anyone got near, it got really scared

Flapping around the garden injured and impaired

Billy would go invisible, so the bird couldn't see

Then untie the string, so then it could be free

So Billy took his honey, he was all ready to go

It was hiding under the trees, so Billy had to fly low

He landed near the bird, it looked all so sad

The string it was all tangled, around its wing pretty bad

He sat and thought, what do I need

To help this bird to be freed

He said, "I'll do it myself, I have to try

We need to help this bird, so it can fly."

Really calm he had to stay

Cos if it felt him it would flutter away

His honey levels were running low

He needed to be quick so he could go

He untied the string, free at last

It flew away very fast

Our job is done, it's in the sky

Everyone waving and shouting goodbye.

CHAPTER 3

Day off

We're having a day off, Billy and me

Thought we'd go on a trip, many sights to see

Boiling hot day I wore my shorts and vest

Billy just sits on my shoulder, when he needs to rest

We went to a park, there were lots of flowers

Billy goes from one to the other, for hours and hours

I just laid down, on the grass

Watching all the people as they pass

It got so hot the sun was burning my lips

So I went and got some juice, and a big bag of chips

Billy gets his food from inside the flower

I'm so hot and sticky now I need a shower

Billy started to be mischievous, he said, "I want to have some fun."

He buzzed around at the burger van, made a lady drop her bun

A man had some rubbish, he went to put it in the bin

Billy buzzed around his head, there was a lake the man fell in

I'm really tired now, off laying in all the heat

Jumped on the bus, looked around, and found myself a seat

The next adventure tomorrow, it could be a really busy week

So me and Billy just for now, need to get some sleep.

CHAPTER 4

Jump

"Help, Billy please," shouted out a mum

Stuck on the ledge of a cliff was David her son

Playing on the top of the cliffs, it was snowing, he had his sledge

He was walking where he shouldn't, over the barriers too near the edge

He lost his footing but he hung on

Held onto the grass but not for long

His friends tried to grab him by his hand

He fell on a ledge but safely he did land

He went over the barriers cos he was dared

Now sitting on a ledge won't jump, too scared

It was only a six foot drop to jump into the sea

But he just couldn't do it, so we went out, Billy and me

He was sitting on the ledge, he was fine not hurt

Just all his clothes were covered in dirt

The sea was calm, there were men waiting in a boat

They threw up a ring, so he would float

We told him to jump and stop being silly

He said he can't, so it's time for Billy

So he took his honey, Billy the bee

His mission was to get David to jump in the sea

Off he went, down the side of the cliff

David was standing there all rigid and stiff

Billy was circling him around in the air

David was going crazy pulling his hair

He was trying to hit Billy with his coat

Then he jumped in the sea and was pulled in the boat

Another successful mission for Billy the bee

We love happy endings, Billy and me.

CHAPTER 5

Puppy Training

Billy got a call, off a girl about her pup

It was really naughty, and chewing things, her mum wants to give it up

He's only 12 weeks old, he's lovely, he's called Bert

Her mum got really angry today, he put a hole in her brand new skirt

She pushed him off her, and made him yelp

Now she needs Billy to try and help

So off we went when her mum was out

So Bert didn't hear her scream and shout

Her mum doesn't really mean no harm

She just wants Bert to be a bit more calm

He was running and falling, it was really funny

So Billy again took his honey

If you shout at a pup, it won't let you near

Billy calmed Bert down, he gently buzzed in his ear

He stopped still, and tilted his head

Then we give him a treat and off he went to bed

Billy stayed with Bert for the rest of day

Buzzing around, showing him the way

The girl was so happy, she couldn't believe

Wiping away happy tears, with her sleeve

When her mum came in, she looked tired and pale

Bert ran up to her, wagging his tail

Now her mum and Bert, they have so much fun

As for me and Billy, that's a job well done.

Chapter 6

Spuds

A shout from a farmer who lives down the road

Someone's stealing his potatoes, they're taking them by the load

We went down to the field, it was half past eight

They go down to the bottom, through the big red gate

It's a big job, Billy, you think you should take it on

He said, "If I don't, and police won't help, all his spuds they'll be gone."

We waited and waited for hours on end

Then this green wagon came round the bend

He got out his cab, after he came up the street

Billy was quick, he flew on his seat

He had his honey, you couldn't see he was there

When he gets back in his cab, Billy would give him a scare

We were hiding down, so we wouldn't be seen

They pick up the spuds with a big red machine

I rang the police and said, "We've solved the case."

Billy in the cab, buzzing around his face

He would've arrested him himself, if he could

The man fell out the door, face down in the mud

The police came, they were just in time

Billy did it again, he solved the crime

Then off we went home, we went through the woods

Farmer was waving thanks for saving me spuds.

CHAPTER 7

Ghost Train

In a ghost train, down at the fair
A cat needed saving, but nobody would dare
It got stuck, in the train's tunnel
How it got there is a bit of a puzzle
They tried to get it out
They screamed and shout
But no matter what they did
They just couldn't get rid

The ride was cancelled, he was set to stay

The fair was losing money, they needed him away

The cat's owner shouted for Billy, he was really worried

You could hear the panic in his voice, so me and Billy hurried

We walked in the tunnel, it was jet black

We walked up the middle of the train track

The further you walked, it got colder and colder

Billy didn't fly, he just sat on my shoulder

Then we heard the cat, it was crying

Billy jumped off my shoulder and started flying

I had a torch, it was shining bright

When the cat saw it, it got a fright

He didn't need his honey, Billy the bee

It was that dark anyway, so you couldn't see

The cat was scared, on the track it clings

Then it heard Billy's tiny wings

Billy didn't need to scream and shout

Little buzz of his wings, and the cat ran out

The cat goes back, where he's from

The fair's happy, the ghost train's back on.

CHAPTER 8

Where's The Milk

Billy got a call, from residents in a street,

Someone's stealing their milk, it's gone on now for a week

They hear the milk float, and the bottles clink

Few hours later there's no milk to drink

No cereal for breakfast, not even tea

This is a job, for Billy the bee

There were residents in the street that never even knew

Cos they never stole them all, was always just a few

So Billy just had to sit and wait

Till he heard them open the garden gate

Then he would sit on the bottle top

Wait till they tried to take it, then give him a shock

The morning has come, now it's time

I don't know if they realised they were committing a crime

He walked up the path, with an untouchable swank

He couldn't see Billy, lots of honey he drank

The milk was on the step, it was in a stand

He went to get it, Billy flew on his hand

He dropped the milk, ran away with pace

Billy kept with him, flying around his face

He ran in a field, there were a few in a tent

There were other boys, it was him they sent

Billy went in the tent, buzzing around

They all ran out screaming, and falling down

So when they stole the milk, we knew where they went

They met their match with Billy, they left and took the tent.

Chapter 9

Saving Beth

Billy got a call, off his bee friend called Beth

She had climbed in some porridge, she had to hold her breath

She got hit in mid air, and fell on the table

She tried to fly away, but she was simply unable

So she's stuck in some porridge, from where she had crawled

Now she needs help, so Billy the bee she called

The people that hit her are very mean

Now she needs to hide, so she can't be seen

They hit Beth, and started to attack

Now she's stuck in some porridge, hoping they don't come back

Billy quickly needed to get around

She was sinking deeper and deeper down

He went to the house and under their door

Then for safety he crawled along the floor

Beth was tiring, it was such a strain

So Billy drank some of his honey again

Up he went, flew past the bin

Looking for the bowl that Beth was in

He looked in one and she was there

He landed on the side, and give her a scare

With his tiny legs he pulled her free

Porridge in her eyes, she couldn't really see

There was a window, he flew through the gap

They were outside now, no turning back

She said that was the worst place she'd ever been

Billy then helped her to get nice and clean

Now she's all fixed, and on the mend

Billy the bee and Beth's friendship will never end.

Chapter 10

How We Met

Me and Billy, we met while I was at school

I had just come out of the swimming pool

Went in the changing room, got ready and got my bag

"Is there something in there for me?" Stood in front of me said this lad

"Well you won't mind if I take a look."

He took my bag and he shook and shook

I said, "Give me my bag back, give me it now."

I could feel the sweat on my brow

He said, "You want your bag, come and take it from me."

Then out of nowhere appeared this bee

It went straight for his face buzzing around

He dropped my bag to the ground

People were laughing, he looked like a fool

He ran straight out the changing room, and jumped in the pool

I went outside for dinner, on my own on the grass

I had my packed lunch, another half hour before class

I had honey and sandwiches, and thought what's just happened was weird

Then the bee that just saved me, suddenly appeared

I looked down at him, at his yellow and black fur

His buzzing is really calming, almost like a purr

He flew on the honey but fell in the pot

Then he just disappeared, believe it or not

I hope he hasn't died was my first fear

Then I heard the noise of his wings, buzzing in my ear

The honey made him invisible, how could that be?

So that's what I called him, Billy the invisible bee

Billy saved me, from the boy's threat

So me and Billy, that's how we met.

www.ingramcontent.com/pod-product-compliance
Lightning Source LLC
Chambersburg PA
CBHW041430040426
42444CB00022B/3489